MANIPULATION SECRETS

Learn the Secrets of Covert Manipulation, How to Identify a Manipulator, NLP, and Proven Manipulation Techniques

By

Jake Bishops

Table of Contents

Introduction 9

Chapter 1: How to Influence People 11

Win People in Your Mind 11

The 6 Standards of Influence 12

    Preferring 14

    Authority 15

    Social Confirmation 15

Weapons of Influence 16

    Reciprocation 17

    Commitment and Consistency 17

    Social Proof 18

    Liking 18

    Authority 19

    Scarcity 19

Chapter 2: What Is Persuasion and NLP and How to Use It 21

Models of Neuro-Linguistic Programming 21

    Strategies 21

    Memory 21

Belief *22*

Motivation *22*

Decision *22*

Learning *23*

Submodalities *23*

Anchoring *24*

Visual Anchors *26*

Auditory Anchors *26*

Kinesthetic Anchors *27*

Trans-derivational Search *27*

Leading Statements *28*

Chapter 3: What Subliminal Messages Are the Best Persuasion and Manipulation Techniques 30

Common Techniques to Use in Manipulation 32

The Advantage of Home Court *33*

The Target Is Always the First One to Speak *33*

The Facts Are Always Changing *34*

They Show Their Negative Emotions with Loud Voices *34*

Not Giving the Target Enough Time to Make Decisions *35*

Criticism and Judgment against the Target *36*

Using Guilt All of the Time *37*

Chapter 4: NLP for success 38

NLP Techniques 38

Meta Model 39
Mirroring 39
Framing 40
Pattern Interruption 40

Manipulation through NLP Techniques 41

The Eye Cues 41
Anchoring 44
Setting the NLP Anchor 46

Chapter 5: Creating Strategies for Manipulation 47

Steps 1 - Define Your Goal(s) 47
Step 2 - Chart the Paths to Success 48
Step 3 - Collect enough Information 49
Step 4 - Identify Opportunities and Threats 51

Opportunities 51
Influence 52
Persuasion 52
Deception 53
Threats 54

Step 5 - Take Action 54

Chapter 6: Self-Confidence and Self-Love 56

Why Do We Need Confidence?..56

    1. *Self-confidence Shows True Acceptance and Self-love* . 57

    2. *Self-confidence and Positivism* 58

    3. *Self-confidence Shows Maturity*....................................58

Actions That Help Develop Self-Confidence 59

    High Self-Confidence 60

    Low Self-Confidence 62

The Effects of Low Self-Confidence 63

Chapter 7: What Is Covert Emotional Manipulation 65

How Will a Manipulator Target? 65

Polishing and Improving Your Manipulation Strategies 65

Applying Various Methods of Manipulation 66

Using Manipulation Techniques on Your Friends and Acquaintances..66

Theories on Successful Manipulation 66

Practice Regularly..67

Take Your Time Expanding Your Skill......................................68

Start Small..68

Be Choosy about Who You Brainwash 69

Be Selective about Phrasing and Actions..................................69

Manipulative Looks and Stares *70*

Shouting Down on Someone or Yelling *71*

Manipulations by Avoiding you at All Means *71*

Preferential or Silent Treatment *72*

Playing on the Emotions *72*

Chapter 8: Victims of Manipulation 74

Three Ways of Becoming the Victim of a Controlling Manipulator 74

   1. Sales Tactics *74*

   2. Working Environment *77*

   3. Personal Relationships *81*

Chapter 9: Identifying Manipulator Types 83

Illustration 84

Harassment and Concealed Manipulation 86

   Internal Symptoms of Concealed Manipulation *89*

Final Thoughts on Manipulation 90

Conclusion 93

© Copyright 2021 by Jake Bishops - All rights reserved.

This Book is provided with the sole purpose of providing relevant information on a specific topic for which every reasonable effort has been made to ensure that it is both accurate and reasonable. Nevertheless, by purchasing this Book, you consent to the fact that the author, as well as the publisher, are in no way experts on the topics contained herein, regardless of any claims as such that may be made within. As such, any suggestions or recommendations that are made within are done so purely for entertainment value. It is recommended that you always consult a professional before undertaking any of the advice or techniques discussed within.

This is a legally binding declaration that is considered both valid and fair by both the Committee of Publishers Association and the American Bar Association and should be considered as legally binding within the United States.

The reproduction, transmission, and duplication of any of the content found herein, including any specific or extended information, will be done as an illegal act regardless of the end form the information ultimately takes. This includes copied versions of the work, physical, digital, and audio unless express consent of the Publisher is provided beforehand. Any additional rights reserved.

Furthermore, the information that can be found within the pages described forthwith shall be considered both accurate and truthful when it comes to the recounting of facts. As such, any use, correct or incorrect, of the provided information will render the Publisher free of responsibility as to the actions taken outside of their direct purview. Regardless, there are zero scenarios where the original author or the Publisher can be deemed liable in any fashion for any damages or hardships that may result from any of the information discussed herein.

Additionally, the information in the following pages is intended only for informational purposes and should thus be thought of as universal. As befitting its nature, it is presented without assurance regarding its prolonged validity or interim quality. Trademarks that are mentioned are done without written consent and can in no way be considered an endorsement from the trademark holder.

Introduction

Manipulation is like an act of seduction where the other is duped for a particular purpose and of personal interest for the manipulator. This appears constantly throughout life and with all types of people, from the youngest to the adults, in all types of vital circumstances that propitiate the achievement of an objective that interests one.

When we talk about manipulation, we cannot only focus on serious cases of psychopathology, but it is in our daily lives:

- **Advertisements** - lead one to wonder where the persuasion ends and the manipulation begins, so that one buys a certain product that one did not intend to buy or that one does not even need.
- **Politicians like Hitler or Mussolini** - manipulated entire populations to follow them in their personal ends.
- **Media** - forgets the objectivity of journalism.
- And a very long etcetera.

Manipulation techniques are used daily and in all kinds of situations, but the problem begins when one does not know how to relate to others without manipulating them or when one is being manipulated without being aware of it.

The basis of manipulation techniques is directly linked to the management of the emotions of others. They tend to use or provoke those that generate more ethical conflicts or try to enhance the personal weaknesses of the person to make it more fickle to influence.

Sometimes, the manipulation can be so subtle that one does not even consider that the decision he/she has made has not been manipulated or influenced by another person, but rather believes that it has been a personal choice. Sometimes we talk about manipulation dynamics in relationships, in work situations, in those friends who always get what they want, or we can talk about politics and marketing strategies.

Manipulation techniques are there, it is even possible that you have manipulated others without being aware of it or yes, to be accepted or to obtain some kind of benefit.

Chapter 1: How to Influence People

At the point when you talk about affecting or manipulating people, our ears liven up at Buffer. The exhortation from Christine Comaford above has that commonplace ring of Carnegie to it. Expel your personality. Default to joy and inspiration. Be inviting to other people.

Win People in Your Mind

- The best way to outwit a contention is to maintain a strategic distance from it.
- Show regard for the other individual's assessments. Never state, "You're off-base."
- If you are incorrect, let it be known rapidly and vehemently.
- Begin agreeably.
- Get the other individual saying, "indeed, yes," right away.
- Let the other individual do a lot of the talking.
- Let the other individual feel that the thought is his or hers.
- Try sincerely to see things from the other individual's perspective.
- Be thoughtful with the other individual's thoughts and wants.
- Appeal to the nobler thought processes.
- Dramatize your thoughts.

- Throwdown a test.

We intend to incorporate the same number of Carnegie standards as we can in the manner that we impart in messages, in remarks, and obviously via web-based networking media. Here are a few models of how our Happiness Heroes practice benevolence, compassion, and seeing things from another person's viewpoint.

Here is my top choice:

Abstain from deceiving features. A staple of Carnegie's strategies includes perceiving the significance of others. Time after time, we overlook this and treat online crowds as effectively controlled rubes. Rather than composing misleading content features that mean to pressure, it's smarter to rehearse interactive features that work for progressively righteous reasons.

The 6 Standards of Influence

Manipulation is frequently described as a type of influence that is neither compulsion nor discerning influence. In any case, this portrayal quickly brings up the issue: Is each type of neither influence that is neither pressure nor balanced influence a type of manipulation? If manipulation doesn't consume the whole intelligent space of influences that are neither sane influence nor intimidation, at that point, what recognizes it from different types of influence that are neither compulsion nor objective influence?

The expression "manipulation" is ordinarily thought to incorporate a component of good disapprobation.

Types of influence like those recorded above are typical of common life. This recognizes them from types of influence depicted as "manipulation" in the unrestrained choice writing. There, the expression "manipulation" normally alludes to radical programming or reinventing of all or a large portion of an operator's convictions, wants, and other mental states. Such worldwide manipulation (as we may call it) is additionally ordinarily envisioned as happening using strongly extra-standard strategies, for example, extraordinary intercession, direct neurological designing, or radical projects of teaching and mental molding. Worldwide manipulation is normally thought to deny its casualty of through and through freedom. This regular instinct drives the "manipulation contention," which tries to guard in compatibilism by asserting that living in a deterministic universe is practically equivalent to having been the casualty of worldwide manipulation.

In any case, this rundown ought to give a sensibly decent feeling of what we mean by "manipulation" in the present setting. It oughtto serve to outline the wide assortment of strategies generally portrayed as manipulation.

Do any of those sound commonplaces? Put another way, Cialdini's rundown could resemble this:

- Reciprocation, for example, Correspondence Norm
- Consistency, for example, Intensification Hypothesis.
- Social confirmation, for example, Social Influence
- Liking, for example, Social Influence (once more)
- Authority, for example, Yale Attitude Change Approach.
- Scarcity, for example, Shortage Principle.

One of the repeating themes from Cialdini's rundown is that of society. The standards of enjoying, authority, and social confirmation all arrange with associations with others: We are convinced by those we like, by those whom we esteem to be authority figures, and by the all-inclusive community. Here are a couple of novel utilizations:

Preferring

One-way people misuse this is to discover approaches to make themselves like you. Do you like golf? Me as well. Do you like football? Me as well. Albeit frequently these are certified, some of the time, they're not.

Enjoying is comparable enough to a consistency that it bears, calling attention to the distinction here. Somebody may state, "Do you like having more guests to your blog?" They aren't searching for an association with you (as in Liking), but instead, they're looking for Consistency. You'll state truly, and in theory, you'll make some harder memories easing off that explanation when you are pitched an item or administration later.

Authority

Something as basic as advising your crowd regarding your certifications before you talk, for instance, expands the chances you will convince the crowd.

Noah Kagan does this for every visitor post he distributes at OK Dork. He composes a fast introduction on how he made the association with the visitor essayist and all the stunning certifications the visitor author has.

Social Confirmation

People will almost certainly say yes when they see others doing it as well. Social proof isn't all terrible. It's one of the fundamental ways we learn throughout everyday life.

Basecamp has an incredible case of social confirmation on their site, demonstrating the wide assortment of regarded customers that utilization the item—and doing as such in an enjoyable, congenial way.

Two others that merit calling attention to are consistency and shortage.

Consistency is simply the one I generally find defenseless to. I recognize a ton with how Parrish depicts the impact: "On the off chance that you request that people express their needs and objectives and, at that point adjust your proposition to that in mind, you make it difficult for people to state no." truly hit the nail on the head for me. Parrish interfaces this to the Ikea impact, how you love your IKEA furniture since you're put resources into it from building it yourself.

Weapons of Influence

The Motivation behind Why – Attaching motivation to a solicitation expands the achievement rate: "I have 5 pages, would I be able to utilize the Xerox machine before you since I'm in a surge" had a triumph pace of 94% vs.60% achievement rate when no 'motivation behind why' was given.

Indicating potential clients, the costliest thing first at that point, working downwards in cost prompts an expansion in the sum spent (as the following items appear to be less expensive in correlation).

Reciprocation

Social Commitments – Humans inalienably disdain being obliged to somebody, to such an extent that frequently a little blessing or favor will prompt a bigger equal reaction. This reality is misused around the world, for example, Rabbit Krishna's who offer an 'endowment' of blossom while requesting gifts (which they will not reclaim). As the beneficiary can't unburden themselves from the subliminal obligation, the social strain to give prompts a higher gift rate than only requesting alone. An Indian general store sold £1000 of cheddar in a couple of hours by welcoming clients to cut their free samples.

Reject and Retreat – This strategy comprises first requesting a significant expense (or an enormous kindness), at that point hanging tight for it to be dismissed, just to line this interest up with a little one, (that you truly needed from the beginning). Statement from a youngster: 'On the off chance that you need a little cat, first request a horse' (Ed).

Commitment and Consistency

We will, in general, stay reliable to our duties, when we have made them (consistency is a socially alluring quality). Concentrates found that when people are inquired whether they would cast a ballot prompted an improved probability to finish. This is the reason it is prescribed to record/verbally express our objectives, as we at that point stand a lot more prominent possibility of adhering to them.

Social Proof

People are influenced by what others do. On a new occasion or circumstance, we look to others in the right manner. This is misused, for instance, in bars or at chapel assortments. The tips/gifts are now and again 'salted' by having cash previously put there or having a sap offer cash to invigorate others to tip. This impact is intensified by how comparable the individual whose activities we are viewing are to ourselves.

Liking

When in doubt, we like to express yes to the solicitation of those we like over those we don't. There are a few key properties that decide our perspective on people: Attractiveness, closeness, praises, contact and co-activity, molding, and affiliation. Concentrates discovered us consequently property qualities, for example, ability, benevolence, trustworthiness, and knowledge to appealing people. It is not co-frequency that 'alluring' political applicants got over multiple times the votes of ugly adversaries.

We like people who behave like us, who are like us, with similar perspectives, interests, convictions, and qualities. We, in this manner, need to discover territories of shared enthusiasm to build affinity and association.

Authority

The more prominent the apparent authority of an individual, the more probable people are to go along (cf the Stanley Milgram tests).

Medical clinics have a 12% day by day mistake rate. This is because medical caretakers and junior specialists will once in a while challenge the choice made by a definitive figure, notwithstanding getting conceivably deadly or odd solicitations.

Scarcity

We are progressively roused to act as if we think we will lose something, then if we are to pick up something. 'Spare £50 per month on...' 'Would not be as successful as you are losing £50 every month on...' A rare thing is more alluring than one that is uninhibitedly accessible.

One situation where you may want to exercise your brainwashing abilities is to make a sale in your business. With the modern world being taken over by entrepreneurs, it can be easy to feel like you might be one of the few who struggle with sales. You can certainly change the face of this experience by learning how to use brainwashing to get people to purchase products from you.

Chapter 2: What Is Persuasion and NLP and How to Use It

Models of Neuro-Linguistic Programming

Strategies

The neuro-linguistic programming theory states that every aspect of the world that we live in is one or a blend of five key strategies. However, over the past decade, psychologists have added two more.

Memory

We have talked about how we use our senses to gather data from the external world. Well, our memories come into play when we are processing these inputs. Notice how you tend to access certain experiences when you are trying to determine whether or not an act is good, neutral, or evil. Moreover, this is the same process utilized when you are learning from a mistake or relishing in the memory of your past achievements. You may be unconscious toward this process, but each and every one of us is always retrieving information from our memory so that we can use it in our decision-making and critical thinking.

Belief

As soon as you process these memories, you establish your own set of interpretations and beliefs. By looking at your experiences, you begin to allow yourself to believe in a higher state that is achievable. With this, you try to aim for something higher. Moreover, you also allow yourself to believe in concepts that will aid your journey in achieving something higher than your current state.

Motivation

The strategical concept of motivation is a combination of memory, belief, and decision. You see, memory is accessed by the individual so that reality is set. Then, you start to compare this set reality to a higher state. You decide which of the options available to you can lead you to this higher state. With all of these combined, you feel motivated to achieve your goals. Motivation is typically different for each individual, as it would depend on one's belief and experience.

Decision

As soon as you realize that there is a higher state that can be achieved, you start to notice the options that are available to you, and you begin to evaluate which of these can help you achieve your goals. You undergo an assessment of what you have experienced in the past, your current situation, and your possible future. After which, you identify how each option can lead you to success. These will serve as your guide on the road to achieving your ideal future. Keep in mind that this strategy is about Test-Operation-Test-Exit (TOTE), which is the strategical model that is traditionally used by psychologists.

Learning

Finally, the strategy of learning incorporates memory, decision, and motivation so that you are much more efficient in achieving your goals. Memory is accessed so that you are much more knowledgeable as to how you can handle the current tasks. Moreover, your past decisions allow you to assess all of your successes and failures. As a result, you'll be inclined to make wiser decisions in the future. Motivation, on the other hand, will prevent you from making the same mistakes. With these strategies, you'll be forced to acquire information on what you already know, what you have experienced in the past, and what you plan on doing.

Submodalities

We have already established that an individual will use their five basic senses, which are gustatory or the sense of taste, visual or the sense of sight, olfactory or the sense of smell, auditory or the sense of hearing, and of course, kinesthetic or the sense of touch; these are referred to as modalities in neuro-linguistic programming. Do note that these modalities are systems of representations that are transmitted and sorted out by the brain. These are the things that affect how we see the world. Furthermore, these modalities can be broken down into submodalities or subjective divisions.

One fair example would be to look at a particular experience and determine whether it is considered a good or bad experience. Depending on what you have experienced in the past, you would say that it is a good experience or a bad one. One person as unimportant can view it, while another would see it as life-changing. Thus, these submodalities play a crucial role in your development as an individual. It affects you on a larger scale, and it transforms your personality based on how you transform past experiences.

Moreover, there are certain techniques you can use to establish an entirely different perspective on unpleasant experiences. This idea does not necessarily mean you have to alter reality or completely ignore it. You are only providing submodalities to subjective experiences so that you are better able to alter your attitude into a more useful one for success and learning.

Anchoring

When it comes to anchoring, you are connecting memories to a stimulus. This stimulus, which is referred to by some as an anchor, becomes a set off to the initial reaction. Do note that a particular anchor does not necessarily have any rational connection to the initial reaction. However, the utilization of these anchors willallow you to stimulate reactions that can change your behavioral patterns toward a condition. The stimuli of sound, sight, smell, taste, and touch are used in neuro-linguistic programming to bring about a particular mindset. This situation can be a memory that you wish to access so that you can change your perspective inlife into something more positive. As soon as the stimulus isinitialized, it elicits a certain mindset with specific emotions and thoughts. This is why hearing an old song makes you feel nostalgicabout your childhood.

In NLP, anchoring becomes useful because you are given a chance to associate certain triggers that you wish to achieve. You are given the power to establish an anchor, as well as create a stimulus and induce a state of mind that is essential for you to achieve success. For example: when someone you love gives you a memento, such as a locket, then this locket becomes the trigger. Moreover, your memories with that person become a state of mind. These two are closely tied together that at times when you look at the particular object, you immediately think about the individual who handed it to you, a resourceful state. These anchors can be visual, kinesthetic, or auditory. You can utilize these as tools to create a mental image that is easily retrievable from your memory so that you are better able to facilitate a response. This tactic improves an individual's critical and subjective point of view of the environment.

You may ask how all of these are essential to dark psychology and the power of manipulation. You need to be able to read them first. If you want to read people, then you would need to have a keen eye as to what their anchors are. Aside from paying attention to how their body reacts to certain things, knowledge of these anchors can facilitate the gathering of information on the one being manipulated.

Visual Anchors

One common misconception about visual anchors is that these are only external. However, visual anchors can be both external and internal. When talking about external visual anchors, we are about what is seen by the naked eye. An internal visual anchor, on the other hand, pertains to the use of our imagination. Going back to our example of the locket, the external anchor is the locket itself, whereas the internal anchor could be a mental image of the person who gave you the locket. Visual anchors can be objects, people, places, or shapes. This is why some things in our life possess sentimental value.

Auditory Anchors

Similar to visual anchors, auditory anchors can also be internal or external. The exact tune or sound that you hear is an auditory anchor that is external, whereas, when you hear the voice in your head, this is more of an internal auditory anchor. Listening to a particular song to help soothe you is an excellent example of an external auditory anchor. Moreover, you can also recall the voice of your big sister calming you and relate it with a fond memory in your childhood so that you are better able to relax.

Kinesthetic Anchors

When talking about internal kinesthetic anchors, we are about imagined actions or gestures received because you did something great. It could be a memory of a hug, handshake, or a pat on the back. Do note that these are all imagined. These are usually associated with a feeling of success or achievement. As for external kinesthetic anchors, these are the actual hugs felt, handshakes made, and the literal pat on the back.

Trans-derivational Search

This kind of search, which is also known as TDS, is a phrase utilized at times when an individual attempts to search for the meaning of ambiguous statements. It is a fundamental human tendency to look for the missing pieces of data from our experiences and memory to provide significance to these incomplete statements. There is a present state of confusion experienced by the individual when the search is being executed; this allows you to experience a trance-like feeling. Neuro-linguistic programming experts can easily put their patients into a trance- like condition or state of hypnosis because of this. You have a better chance of manipulating another person by taking advantage of the window at which they are experiencing TDS. This is made possible by mentioning ambiguous and incomplete statements.

Leading Statements

If you want to utilize the concepts under TDS, then you should master how to create leading statements. These statements must elicit the feeling of uncertainty from the other person. It must be ambiguous enough to trigger the imagination to try to complete the statement. Furthermore, your leading statement should initiate a mood without providing its full explanation. As a result, the brain will be tempted to process the information provided and to find its missing pieces. Here are some great examples of what your leading statements should be.

"What you said yesterday." This particularly vague statement will allow the mind to wander and retrace everything that has happened within the set parameters of the statement, which is yesterday. The individual that you are trying to manipulate will then consider everything relevant to the discussion. They will consider the period and the words you have said, and then they will search internally for the idea that will make your initial statement complete. Their mind will start to go through a certain process of elimination until they can narrow down to the actual meaning of the statement.

"The different shades of paint." If you utter this statement to an individual, that person's mind will start to explore all the possible shades of paint. Your leading statement was able to set the parameters and scope, which are the shades of paint, without fully divulging the exact answer as to which shade. This will lead the other person to wonder which shade you are referring to.

Chapter 3: What Subliminal Messages Are the Best Persuasion and Manipulation Techniques

One thing that we need to take a few minutes to note when it comes to manipulation is that there is positive manipulation and negative manipulation. These are going to utilize the same kinds of techniques along the way, but the intention behind them is going to be slightly different, and this is how we get each kind.

We have spent some time looking at the negative manipulation and how it is going to try and harm the person who is the target. As long as the manipulator can get what they want and can use the target as a tool, they are going to do so—and it doesn't matter to them whether the target gets harmed in the process or not. As long as the manipulator sees themselves as the winner, or as the one in control, they will be happy.

Now, there is also a type of manipulation that is seen as more positive. This is going to use the same kinds of techniques that we can see with negative manipulation, but it is going to work with better intentions. The manipulator in this kind is still going to work to get what they want from the target, but they have a conscience here, and they don't want to harm the other person. Often, this kind is going to be beneficial to both parties or will be more beneficial to the target than the manipulator.

For example, if a family tries to use manipulation to get their child to go to addiction recovery from alcohol or another substance, this is still seen as a form of manipulation. Still, it is done for the good of the target, rather than to cause them harm. If you go into a car lot to purchase a car, the salesperson is likely going to use some of the techniques of manipulation and even persuasion to make the sale.

Sometimes, the manipulation is not going to be such a bad thing. Yes, we are using techniques that may be considered bad or unethical, but it is done with the health and safety, and even the benefit, of the target in mind the whole time. This is a manipulator because the person is doing the techniques to get something that they want in life—but in the positive manipulation, the point is not just to help out the manipulator but also to help out the target in the process.

Keep in mind that with manipulation, whether it is positive or negative, we are dealing with the same techniques. But you can use the same techniques to help out if you plan to work with positive manipulation instead.

So, the basic difference that we are going to see when it comes to positive and negative manipulation is how the target is treated in the process. The manipulator is going to win in either scenario. But in positive manipulation, the target is allowed to win and benefit as well. Then, when we are looking at negative manipulation, we are going to see that the manipulator is the onlyone who wins. The target is going to be used and often harmed in the process as the manipulator gets what they want.

Common Techniques to Use in Manipulation

In reality, there are so many different techniques that a manipulator is going to try and use against you, that it can be hard to know how to defend against them all. Pretty much any technique that the manipulator can use to get you to act in the manner that they want to benefit themselves, whether it is with you doing it willingly or by force, is going to be fair game when wemeet with a manipulator. With that in mind, there are a few examples of the techniques that a lot of manipulators like to work with to see the results that they need with their target—and some of these common techniques of manipulation are going to include:

The Advantage of Home Court

When someone is trying to manipulate a new target, they will try to use any method possible to gain the upper hand in that situation. This is why the manipulator may decide it is a good idea to do the meeting at their home, in their office, or somewhere else the manipulator is familiar with, and that the target has no idea about.

On the other hand, the victim is going to be really out of their element. They are happy that the manipulator wants to meet with them, and may think that it is very friendly that the manipulator is willing to pick the place, seeing this as a hospitable thing to do. But in reality, it is all to the advantage of the manipulator, just like anything else they do. It helps them to get the upper hand against the target from the very beginning.

The Target Is Always the First One to Speak

This is something that you will see with sales quite a bit. From here, they can get a good idea of your weaknesses and strengths. This type of questioning will have a hidden agenda, and we may be able to find it in other places of our lives, such as in personal relationships and the workplace.

The Facts Are Always Changing

Whenever you are talking to a manipulator, you will find that the facts are never going to be the same each time you bring them up. And if the manipulator thinks that changing up the facts will make their target look bad and make themselves look good, then they are going to be even more eager to do this. They will deny that plans were made. They will just show a bias towards the side that works for them. They may blame the target for messing things up and not getting things right. They will make up their excuses, lie, and deform and twist the truth as much as they want to confuse the target and get what they want in the process.

They Show Their Negative Emotions with Loud Voices

Another tactic that the manipulator may try to use is to raise their voice to help show off some of their negative emotions. This is going to happen many times during a discussion to show a form of aggressive manipulation and to make the target worry about whether they have upset the manipulator or not. The assumption here with the manipulator is that if they are then able to project the voice and make sure that it comes across loud enough. They can add some negative emotions to this, then the victim is going to be tense and fearful, and will give the manipulator exactly what they want in the process.

To go along with the aggressive emotions and voice, it is common for the manipulator to make sure that every part of their body language is used to get the message across to the target as much as they can. They will have strong body language that is meant to intimidate as much as possible, show anger, and move the hands around to showcase that the target needs to back off and do what the manipulator wants.

Not Giving the Target Enough Time to Make Decisions

This is one that manipulators of all kinds, even those who are salespeople, are going to use to get what they want. They will present some options to their target and then will limit how much time the target is going to get to make that decision. The hope here is that the target is going to jump right on what the manipulator is suggesting to them, without worrying about doing research or thinking it through. Of course, the position that the manipulator is trying to push is going to be something that benefits the manipulator, and will maybe cause harm to the target.

The idea of giving just a little bit of time to the victim to let them decide on things has been used in many forms of manipulation. We can see this as a tactic that is used in sales and negotiations. When you start to apply this kind of tension and control how long the target gets to make decisions, the hope here is that the target will give in to whatever the aggressor is demanding.

Criticism and Judgment against the Target

This is a type of behavior that can be distinct in several methods from some of the other tactics that we have talked about so far for manipulation. In this one, we are going to see that the manipulator spends a lot of time joking and picking on their target, in the hopes of lowering the confidence and self-esteem of the target as much as possible. By constantly dismissing, marginalizing, and ridiculing the victim, the manipulator is going to be successful at keeping their victim off-balance, while helping the manipulator to stay superior along the way.

Often, the aggressor is going to like this tactic because it is going to deliberately foster the idea that something is going wrong with the victim, and that no matter how hard the victim works, they are never good enough to meet those impossibly high standards that the manipulator is going to set up from the start.

Of course, the thing here is that the manipulator hyper focuses on the bad and ignores all the good things that come with the target. They do this because, if the target realizes there are some good factors about them, then they would ignore the manipulator. With this tactic, the manipulator will learn how to focus just on the negative things about their target (and we all have some negative traits), and then never offer constructive help on how to make it better. This shows that they are doing this just to make the target feel bad.

We think that we are making them suffer some when we don't give them our attention all the time and that by making them sweat it out for a bit; we are more likely to get what we would like.

The silent game is a head game, where the manipulator can use silence as a form of leverage against the victim.

Using Guilt All of the Time

The manipulator can then make you feel bad for something, even if that situation is not your fault, and finds it easier to coerce the target to give in and agree to the demands they give, even when these demands are unreasonable, to make the guilt go away.

Chapter 4: NLP for success

NLP Techniques

Neuro-Linguistic Programming (NLP) tells you that emotions and experiences is what guides people in their view of the world. That what you currently see is not the real world, but a distorted representation based on your beliefs, perceptions, values, and other variables. Use NLP strategies will help you build on aspects of your life and help you improve your quality and understand how people work. Discover how to use these NLP methods to improve the communication skills and emotional intelligence that you can use to control your life and mind.

The technique of anchoring in NLP is necessary to pull up a certain emotion or to place you into a certain mental state. That can also be used on yourself, or someone else. This works by integrating emotion with a physical movement and is dubbed the anchor laying. For instance, if you decided to pull the excitement feeling, then you would start by thinking about times you've been euphoric. You would like to tell the account of what went on in yourhead that led to this moment. Talk about how it feels and goesinto agreat deal of detail. Remember the moment, the emotions.

First, keep in your right hand your left index and middle fingers. There are two squeezes you want to give them. Talk about your special moment on the second squeeze and strive to add the sensation. Describe once again how you feel, how you think, and twice click your hands. Let the warm feeling double when you click the second time. Do it five times. You could use those gestures later to regain your feeling of happiness. You could use a quick touch of the arm to secure them if you were to do this to another man.

Meta Model

The methodology of the meta-model of NLP is often used to make you understand the concerns of other individuals. It could also be used to support others better understand their issues. The aim is to dismantle the discussion, help you achieve the root cause of the issue, and fix it. The response is consciously or unconsciously understood when someone has a question, but often the simplest solution is something that they do not like. The lack of uncertainty allows the crisis to persist, anticipating that there will finally be a new solution. You can help them develop a way by deconstructing the way someone explains their question.

Mirroring

One of the most relevant NLP strategies you should learn is mirroring. It will be very beneficial to be good at mirroring, as it is hard to hate someone who knows how to do this act. It is the replication of the individual you interact with that individual's behaviors. Subtle and typically subconscious, this simulation is complete. Copying somebody's speech patterns, body language, vocabulary style, speed, rhythm, pitch, voice, and volume are ways that you can do this.

Framing

The technique of NLP framing is used to affect the increase or decrease of the emotional feeling significantly. It's a great way to use it, along with most of the others. You're going to experience good and bad moments in life. These should enable you in your life to be able to learn and grow. Nonetheless, memories have no feelings connected to them. Such separation is because in different parts of the brain, there exist memories and thoughts. So at present, you will experience feelings, and then you will be able to remember them. The hippocampus is the brain part that is responsible for long-term memory storage. The amygdala is the brain's portion that regulates feelings. The amygdala will give you a quick little reminder of the feelings you feel when you recall a memory from the hippocampus. Just because of that, the sensation that is important to a specific memory can be modified.

Pattern Interruption

Interruption of the pattern is often used to preserve words in a listener's subconscious mind. One great technique to pair with others is this technique. To do this, you have to draw the thoughts of the listener into a series or pattern form. When the model gets out of control, before finishing the form, you take them out of the template for a critical juncture. The unconscious mind of the listener is supposed to embody the pattern, while the conscious mind is overwhelmed at the moment. You can change the way you think, look at the past, and view your life with a new way of thinking by learning NLP. It can help to improve your communication skills and enhance your emotional intelligence. It's a way to regulate your mind, which helps you handle your life better.

Manipulation through NLP Techniques

Getting to understand NLP techniques will help you in manipulating people for a positive impact on your life.

The Eye Cues

It is necessary to calibrate your NLP eye accessing signals while communicating with someone to ensure that you perceive the signals appropriately.

Left-handed people tend to turn left and right, but note that they don't depend on their left/right-handed choice.

When eyes move to the right side, it means Visual Construction (VC) - The person is taking a picture about something they have not seen. While there may be some aspects of the image from memory, other elements are being created (envisioned).

When the eyes move up and to the left means Visual Remembered (VR) - Here the person is recalling an image of anything.

When the eyes move on the right, there is Auditory Constructed (AC) - Here, the person imagines something they've never seen before. This is likely, in my opinion, the least experienced access cue.

When the eyes move on the left means there is Auditory Recalled (AR) - Here, a sound from memory is recalled by the user.

When the eyes move down or right, Kinesthetic (K) means that the consumer relies on an internal emotion. When the eyes move down and left Auditory Digital (AD) means in their ear, the client listens to the conversations going on from the inside.

When you have mastered the list for processing NLP eye signals, the best thing is to look at people for some time to see if their facial expressions make any sense to you.

For example, when people keep speaking about their new ride and how to flash it was, they kept glancing up and left, implying that they were taking photos. Does this seem highly likely to be so?

But just be vigilant with your assumptions: If a right-handed individual says they have submitted a letter to you, but their eyes go up and left, most people would assume they're lying. You can't know for sure, of course, without measuring. All this knowledge informs you (guessing you know by gazing up and left they recall visual recollections) is they're creating an illustration. We can make up a picture of them uploading the letter or imagine anything completely different. They may not have published the letter by themselves or imagine the message being published.

In this case, an easy way to configure might be to ask what you believe they will understand and see whether or not their eyes are heading the same way. And note that this has to be done slowly and informs you only if the picture was remembered or created.

It takes a while to start noticing these often subtle signals and ignore the noise when you start trying to watch NLP eye accessing signals. When projecting the image with a much more visible look, the eyes of many people can move very quickly to reach a memory. For example, when you ask someone to remember their tenth birthday, they'll certainly look up and on the left side quickly, look at a point on their timeline and see the picture there.

Such accesses sometimes occur in pairs, and the logic of what someone has to do to answer the question is worth considering. For example, what is likely to be the eye movement when you ask somebody to reflect about a moment when they feel at ease?

Will the individual react by looking down and to the right to the feeling (K)?

Or are they trying to imagine the location they felt the ease (VR)?

The response is they're going to do both, almost certainly. They will probably reach the emotion, then just go back to their memories, searching for and imagining the corresponding moment.

Also, importantly, if you begin to ask intelligent questions about the images and sounds that they make as they think, you will finally find somebody who will pledge falsely that they are not making any images in their minds.

You may find that their eyes move exactly as you would be expecting when you ask them the important questions. You may be concerned about what that means.

Okay, first of all, you should note that they are not lying-they are just dealing with what they're aware of, but they are forming mental images.

Anchoring

While using the anchoring technique; the concept is simple, you should get a client or consumer into a particular mental condition, and establish a relationship with it so that the condition can be re-activated at will.

In this post, we're going to deal with the more delicate NLP anchoring strategies you can do in a corporate environment, instead of the type of anchoring that is often used with NLP customers in which you can create a very strong state and continue reaching it purely because the client is happy to follow your instructions.

There are four skills needed in a covert method of anchoring:

- Connect a powerful union
- Recognize when and how to set the anchors
- Anchor the state as precisely as possible
- Fire the anchor if necessary
- Connecting to a powerful union

First, determining which state is being anchored is critical.

When you try to sell, probably you would like your customer to be in a desirable buying state. The easiest method of accessing a system is to make the customer identify when they were in that position: "Do you remember a time when you first saw something and decided you had to have it?" "Have you ever seen something did an impulse buying?" These kinds of questions pressure the customer to remember a time that suits the state and to activate it.

This is important for the effectiveness of your NLP anchoring strategies. Other strong states that you might want to have connections with also include anger about your competitors, transparency, and obstinacy if you have come to see a friend who wants to ignore them.

Setting the NLP Anchor

Some NLP anchor strategies work by having the consumer access some of their memories. The ideal time to anchor the system is to reach the memory-connected state. So have a close look at the eyes and watch every small motion of the body. When they simply fall off or even calm or even become sensitive and enthusiastic in some situations, this will be the time to start putting the anchor.

Chapter 5: Creating Strategies for Manipulation

Steps 1 - Define Your Goal(s)

This is the objective of your deception technique. Without an objective, you run the risk of pointlessly manipulating people. One important consideration for your goals is to decide if they are something you really want to accomplish. There is no point in saying that your goal is to rule the world if you are not willing to make an effort; who wants that kind of power, anyway?

It is also better to define goals to which there is already a clear path. Take the target and break it down. The first thing you might need is management expertise.

Career success is not the only type of goal for which this methodology works.

You could set the goal of carving a niche at work that gives you more free time and allows you to work with less stress. You could set the goal of seeking a caring partner. It doesn't matter the target itself, as long as you really want it.

Don't forget to set a date for your goal as well. Now take note of all your goals, long-term and short-term, large and small, and order them right away.

Remember your targets every single day. You do this by concentrating your attention on a mission. Think of a time when you reached a high level of achievement at work, school, or college. Think about what it takes to do something that makes you proud of yourself. Was it just a modest number of hours, or did it include going the extra mile? Were you dreaming about the project night and day, running it through your brain until you went to sleep and structuring it in your mind? Of course, you were. That is exactly what made the difference.

Through concentrating your attention on a mission, you have devoted all your energy to a high level of achievement. The more attention you have paid to deception, the more you are going to be able to gain and the more likely you are to succeed. Of course, it is also best if you keep all of your ambitions a secret for now.

Step 2 - Chart the Paths to Success

Now that you have the targets, and you have planned how to achieve them, it is pretty easy to find a path to success. If your goal is promotion, you are going to need a manager to support you. If your goal is to find a loving partner, you are going to have to find someone suitable and convince them to get married.

Consider alternative paths to success as well. If you want to take the position of your supervisor, there might be a way for them to get fired or they could be hired in another position, leaving a vacancy open for you.

Map as many directions as you can and find all the options for now.

Once you have done this, it is time to set up the parties involved. Who would be in charge of the decision-making process of your promotion? Who are the potential contenders? How is the information flowing between these people?

In the case of promotion, your strategy of manipulation should be to ensure that the people who have the power to promote you and your brand will want to do so. Did you see the movie Inception? Unfortunately, it is not an option to actually hack into someone's dreams. You need to start understanding their goals and behavior to manipulate your target.

Step 3 - Collect enough Information

Consider the objectives of the people you need to influence—those who will decide whether or not you will be promoted. Note down all their activities from now on, and as much of their previous behavior as possible. Look for patterns and try to relate each of their actions to what you see as their goals. Then look for ways they don't align and reassess their goals to see what matches.

Get to know all the parties involved, including those who have the power to promote you, your competitors, and anyone on the trajectory of your path to success. Include their goals in your notes, record their actions, spot patterns and link them to their goals. Keep the notes organized with all this information and hide it from everyone.

The goal here is to give your brain as much information as possible. Only visualize the brain as a tool again. It has the greatest chance of producing the right outcomes (actions) if it has access to the best inputs (information) and the more you can logically arrange this information, the easier it will be to make smart decisions rather than irrational instinct-based decisions.

After a while, say a few days, you need to start building a picture. Take a little more time if you feel like you need it. Nonetheless, you don't need to have a complete understanding of the situation to begin the next stage of gathering information, which is to recognize the key figures amongst those you are observing. These may well be the ones who have the power to promote you.

You will continue to gather information indefinitely, even as you begin to manipulate others. Make it a habit, and you will improve your speed and accuracy in identifying the expectations and behavioral patterns of others.

Focus on understanding where the power lies, how the parties involved make their decisions, and try to identify what causes them to take action. Please relate this back to your own goals.

Step 4 - Identify Opportunities and Threats

This is where the time has come to use your brain. Every day, you will talk about your ambitions and develop a deeper understanding of the dynamics of your scenario.

Opportunities

Remember the goal you set yourself. So note that your main goal is to want the people in charge of your appointment to support you. What did you learn about their goals? Consider a standard example to be that they want to achieve good numbers—they want to improve the efficiency of your company by increasing their profits.

Relate what you learned about the parties in the scope of your goals back to the paths you mapped out. Begin using that information to determine the likelihood of success in each scenario. Is it more likely that your current team leader is going to be fired or promoted? Weigh up the options against each other.

Suppose you have a reason to believe that your current team leader is under-performing, and you want them to be terminated rather than promoted in their line of duty. In this instance, you need to be careful about timing. The right opportunity will present itself, and when it happens, you need to be in pole position.

Influence

As a candidate in pole position, you are considered to have the most power to help the potential new supervisors (those who would appoint you) achieve their goals. You have even learned that your current boss, the team leader, is facing the sack. This is almost definitely because they are considered to lack the power to help their direct subordinates accomplish their goals. They haven't been sacked yet, though, and this could be for several reasons. They may not have had enough opportunity to prove themselves, or their bosses may not be convinced that you are the best substitute.

Persuasion

Forget going to those with the power to promote you and giving an epic speech about why you are the perfect candidate to be the next team leader. This is not a Hollywood movie. More to the point, the universe is not just going to bend to your request if you ask for it.

Deception

What you can do is act to control the flow of information that hits the subordinates of your employer. The goal, in this case, is to lower their opinion of the authority of your boss and get your boss fired quicker.

The ways you could do this are too many to count. How close are you to the people you need to influence?

Just consider, who do they listen to? Possibly someone on their team. Maybe someone who you are observing. Now you have the opportunity, far enough from yourself, to indirectly influence people directly above your boss.

To recap, this applies to someone approximately your age, working for a team at the same level as your own, who depends on the actions of your colleagues. Immediately begin profiling this individual, their goals and actions.

Bear in mind that this is a hypothetical example, but it gives you an idea of the kind of person you might be able to influence. You will have to analyze your own situation and develop a strategy based on these ideas.

Remember that so much of what is involved in successful manipulation is choosing who to control. You are likely to exploit everyone at some point, to some degree. Right now, you are formulating a plan to exploit a specific situation by exceptional means.

Threats

A potential hazard is that the manager can regain his prestige (perceived power) and escape the danger zone. Remember, anything that may help to interrupt your path to success is a potential threat.

Always look for threats and use the same principles to avert them. Also, act in secrecy to reduce the power of any faction that tries to undermine your plans.

Step 5 - Take Action

Setting the threat aside, refocus on the current example. There, an excuse has emerged to establish a deception. It may well be the case that you have a close relationship with the designated person to facilitate the flow material, in which case it may be possible to conspire. If your manager is truly useless, your task team is genuinely focused on improving the performance of your staff, and your objective is to see this happen, you may potentially agree to work together to promote any knowledge that will damage the reputation of your manager.

You have admitted to another human that you want to conspire. This will have an effect on your reputation and your trustworthiness.

Your partner may change their mind, in which case you will have sabotaged your opportunity to trick them by disclosing your ambitions.

Your partner may change the plan to meet their own goals and undermine your strategy.

For deceit, you are just running the risk of being found out yourself, and it is quite easy to try and lie, which you can reasonably deny if necessary.

For the purposes of this example, say that you are on friendly terms with this person and that you can eat lunch or have coffee with them approximately once a week. Show active interest by asking questions. Add in questions about their job with a natural, personal interest in the subject. Try to focus on pursuing lines of conversation that they are willing to talk about. There is a good chance that this will be related to their interests, which will be linked to their objectives.

Chapter 6: Self-Confidence and Self-Love

Self-confidence is a very important skill, and it gives you the ability to judge your own personal and social standing by your environment and also gain great satisfaction out of it.

Many factors influence self-confidence such as work environment, upbringing, as well as the drive or the level of commitment and enthusiasm towards pursuing a cause. Self-confidence is an essential element in developing and improving business ties as well as your personal life.

Just like the popular saying reminds us, as you begin the journey of your professional life, always have high confidence in the abilities you possess because you have yet to prove your abilities.

This saying has been in circulation as far back as the evolution of modern human society, yet the context couldn't be more accurate than it is today. More so than ever, in the present times that we live in, which are very competitive, self-confidence becomes a great asset, a source of strength, as well as self-sustenance for us.

But first, let's talk about self-confidence, why we need it, and how important it is in our lives.

Why Do We Need Confidence?

Knowing your strength and being confident about it can help you draw in courage and firm determination when things get difficult in life.

Self-confidence helps provide perspective and gives you the courage to carry on when everyone else might view the road ahead or the task at hand to be almost impossible to carry out in the required time.

Confident people can see and recognize what their limitations are and understand how to make up for their limitations with strength and resolve.

All that said, what you should understand is that self-confidence basically depends on your ability to handle actions, so let's talk briefly about the actions that can help in developing self-confidence.

1. Self-confidence Shows True Acceptance and Self-love

People with low self-confidence will mostly rely on the acknowledgment of others to make them feel important or get a sense of pride in themselves.

Self-confident people don't need to get anybody's approval before they feel happy or proud of whom they are. Self-confidence will help you realize or develop an attitude that no matter what challenges you face, or how difficult things get, you have promised yourself that you will always be there for yourself. It is like an unconditional acceptance of who you are.

2. Self-confidence and Positivism

Negativity or a negative mental attitude is toxic to both the physical and emotional well-being of the body. It can also affect the people around us and lead to us pushing them away.

Nobody likes to hang around someone who always blames others for their own mistakes yet will never see their error, or ways to improve.

Self-confident people are typically optimists because they are very confident in themselves, their skills, and their abilities because they think positively and are not easily thrown off-track. They are confident about their course and are sure of succeeding, therefore they don't allow anything to hinder them or worry about negativity.

3. Self-confidence Shows Maturity

When we pay too much attention and get too engrossed in the opinions of other people, we hinder our own path to happiness. When we start caring more about what we want and what we think and let our opinions and decision guide us, then we can enjoy life better in ways we planned to, or the way we want to live it.

One of the major signs of adolescent age is interest and expectations. According to the American Academy of Child and Adolescent Psychiatry (AACAP), adolescents usually appear sad, tearful, and mostly irritable, and there is a decrease in activities they used to be interested in.

They become very sensitive to how people feel about or perceive them.

Self-confident people are usually more emotionally mature, and emotionally mature people are mentally healthy, make better rational decisions, are well attuned, and display a highly positive mental attitude towards themselves, their work, and other people around them.

Actions That Help Develop Self-Confidence

Self-confidence does better in an environment where you receive constructive feedback, while the focus always remains on the positive.

As a confident person working in such an environment, you will be able to practice your skills and abilities far and above expectations. Meaning, you will be opportune to set goals, move beyond past mistakes, and learn new and exciting things.

Meanwhile, an environment where the expectations are impractical and you are always in comparison with others can gravely impede your self-confidence. When people are set as rivals to go against each other according to their performance in the game of numbers, self-confidence is harder to find.

Such circumstances can force you to develop or nurture a competitive mentality that is rather unhealthy. By making use of unjust and iniquitous means to achieve success, you could become ruthless in judging your self-performance, taking after unworthy people as role models, and even underestimating or doubting your capabilities.

Such an atmosphere will create a workplace that is basically unhealthy due to the stress and pressure to outdo someone else's performance, instead of combining your energy as a team and work together while you help and assist each other to succeed. Some organizations actually do practice such a method of pitting staff against each other and it works well. However, it peaks for some time, but most assuredly crashes.

High Self-Confidence

The approach people with high self-confidence employ to tackle problems is usually different from that of other people. They perceptually understand that building relationships is important and therefore, they have a knack for meeting new people, making new friends, and they get to share ideas and learn new things. This quality that they possess is one of the main reasons that they are so likable. Additionally, these highly self-confident people are always prepared to engage in conversations that highlight and grant mutual respect and equal importance to everyone that participated in it.

Another point about people who have high self-confidence is that they are fond of expressing what they think, as well as their ideas in the presence of others. This is because they are secure emotionally to the point that they can easily handle constructive criticism and rebuff the emotional ones. Meanwhile, that is not to say they are arrogant—quite the opposite, they are open and they present everyone with the opportunity to air their views. Nonetheless, they are courageous enough to hold on to their decisions against all the antagonism to their ideas, especially when they believe and are convinced that they are doing the right thing or are on the right track.

Once you have made a decision and it is set in motion, there are two possible outcomes, which are that you have either made the right decision (success) or you made the wrong one (failure). But what distinguishes confident people from others is that when they succeed, they don't throw it in the faces of all those detractors.

Also, highly self-confident people are humble enough to admit to their mistakes and use that opportunity to learn from their failures. They have an objective mindset and approach with regards to both failure and success. That characteristic makes people with self-confidence respectable as well as lovable.

Low Self-Confidence

People who have low self-confidence have an awfully harsh and judgmental view of themselves, which when compared to the highly self-confident people means they are separated by a very wide gap.

People with low self-confidence are susceptible to making emotional decisions instead of thinking rationally. They are more of the "let me stay in my corner" type in place of meeting new people, making new friends, and sharing new ideas. They avoid meeting new people or having company.

People with low-confidence are inclined to feel that they have nothing new, constructive, or consequential to contribute to any process. All these feelings combined with low self-worth and the total denial or avoidance of accepting changes make people with low self-confidence very prone to be undervalued and mistreated.

People with low self-confidence are mostly hesitant to share their views, thoughts, and opinions about things because they think they might be publicly mocked for their views. Naturally, it meanstheir past interactions and experiences with others have little to no impact in enhancing their self-value and self-confidence in any way, therefore their views remain the same about their importance and productivity.

Like we mentioned earlier about the productive environment, this is where it comes into play. Everyone is bound to learn from their environment. The kind of people you meet and the type/quality of discussions you engage in with them directly affect and influence your self-confidence. On one hand, people who are very self-confident mix and interact with others and learn from those from who they can learn. On the other hand, low confident people believe they can't be who they are and that they will remain undervalued no matter what they try.

The Effects of Low Self-Confidence

People need role models who they can look up to and idolize as a compass to guide themselves and measure their own talents and skills, achievements, as well as compare their progress to help them constantly improve themselves. That is exactly how people who are self-confident behave.

High self-confident people choose to interact with others, and in that process, they share their views publicly to gain new perspectives; they keep improving on their skills, and they expand their knowledge constantly.

When people stop doing exactly that, what happens then? Well, without an anchor in their lives to hold them and stabilize them when they are drifting away, and without a model to tether on, they begin to lose focus. Without interaction with society, people will become extremely self-centered and only think about what concerns them, and it will be even more evident in how they take criticism. Everything will appear personal, and even when constructive criticism is aired about their work, it will be assumed to be a personal attack.

The effect of low self-confidence will make people with such personalities think that they are less talented with inferior skills and abilities to handle and complete any assigned task. They feel unworthy to receive compliments and be appreciated. It gets even worse when honest compliments are given for their efforts—it becomes a surprise or shock to them; hence they tag it as false, pretentious, or fake appreciation.

Chapter 7: What Is Covert Emotional Manipulation

How Will a Manipulator Target?

Human beings have various personality traits and types such as warm, passionate, adventurous, loyal and dependable, idealistic, analytical, fun-loving personalities, and many others. Our personality traits are greatly influenced by the biochemical processes ongoing in our bodies. These processes affect how we behave at a given time, making some persons have unpredictable natures and sudden mood swings. Despite all these inconsistencies of the human characters and lives, you still need to learn ways to manipulate and persuade people to get what you want from them.

There are various ways of manipulating a person through persuasion, but you can persuade and influence using your body language and manners of speech respectively. Let us look at some ways to manage and control people like:

Polishing and Improving Your Manipulation Strategies

You can clean your skills for effective manipulation of others through mastering the art of public speaking, theatrical displays, creating parallels and correspondences, exhibiting charismatic traits by displaying self-confidence, and learning from the experts.

Applying Various Methods of Manipulation

Getting what you want, will not be possible if you do not know how to use some techniques of manipulating people like using rationality and logic to present your requests to a person, you can even act like a scapegoat and the victim in dangerous situations. These tactics will subconsciously compel your target to give you what you desire without any restraint. Another way to get what you want from a person is by using a bribing pattern like offering a person something in exchange for what you want from him or her.

Using Manipulation Techniques on Your Friends and Acquaintances

Your friends and acquaintances are the best persons to manipulate to get whatever you want. This is because they must have known you and your personality traits and probably despite your faults will continue to stick to you no matter what happens. To achieve this, you will play on their emotions because your friends should have feelings for you, and most importantly, they commit to help you and make you happy or comfortable if it is in their power to do it. Play on their conscience by reminding them how you have been helpful in the past, and this will motivate them to offer you whatever you desire.

Theories on Successful Manipulation

If you get caught, you will not only completely blow your chances at success in that conversation, but you could end up spoiling your reputation. People do not tend to take lightly this type of situation, as no one likes the idea of being under mind control or brainwashing. To avoid this type of disaster, you need to know how to prevent yourself from getting caught. Getting caught can potentially destroy your success at mind control, as well as any relationships you have used this strategy in. When people catch wind that you are attempting to brainwash them, or that you have effectively done so, they will no longer trust you and this mistrust will spread across your network extremely quickly. People do not appreciate being subjected to brainwashing and mind control, and so they do not want to know that someone they have grown to trust is using it on them.

Practice Regularly

The more you practice, the stronger your mind control game is going to become. You want to make sure that you practice often, preferably in every single conversation you have. Even if you don't actually want anything significant from someone, knowing how to get them to say or do certain things you want will help you practice brushing up on your technique. It could be something as easy as getting someone to touch a certain area on their body, say something in particular, or do anything else small and seemingly unimportant. The more you learn to use these techniques to get what you want, the better.

Take Your Time Expanding Your Skill

It cannot be stressed enough how important it is for you to slow down when it comes to practicing your skill. It may seem like a good idea to embrace many of these techniques at once and create a conversation that will help you get what you want, but this can lead to you being caught, quickly. When you put this type of pressure on yourself in a conversation without having any practice, you essentially infuse the conversation with a lot of unnatural and uncomfortable feeling. This is because you are not practiced at the techniques, so you are attempting to recall them and use them on the spot, and you are doing it with too many at once. People are going to see through you, and they are going to catch you in the act.

Start Small

Sometimes, starting with large goals is honorable. When it comes to learning how to use mind control and not getting caught in the process, it is actually inefficient and an excellent way to get caught, quickly. The best thing you can do is start small with things that are seemingly unimportant and irrelevant. This allows you to practice getting people to say yes or do what you want them to do, with very little pressure on the situation overall. Once you get regular results in getting your smaller goals met, you can start practicing getting larger goals met. This will give you the best opportunity to really get natural in your talent and feel confident when it comes to setting out larger goals and accomplishing them.

Be Choosy about Who You Brainwash

You must be choosy about who you brainwash. Remember, just as you have the opportunity to learn about mind control, so do others. Many people in this day and age are somewhat knowledgeable about the art of mind control. While they may not be masters of it, they may have general knowledge around some tactics such as deceit and manipulation. You must learn to identify those who are more likely to comply with your attempts and those who are more likely to be resistant to mind control.

Be Selective about Phrasing and Actions

You must be careful about the phrasing you use and the actions you carry when you are using mind control strategies. If you use the wrong phrasing, are too forceful or obvious in your phrasing, or have fidgety or otherwise uncontrolled physical movements, you are more likely to be caught. People will recognize that you have something "off" about you and will be less likely to trust you or believe you. This means that you are going to ruin your attempts and even more people will be less likely to believe you because mind control and manipulative types of reputations tend to be exposed and shared on a mass level to prevent other people from becoming manipulated. You need to be very careful in your actions and phrasing, ensuring that you are intentional and that you are behaving in a way that is not going to expose you and let others know what you are doing.

- What are some of the motivations of a manipulator?
- The key to manipulation is using the goals of others to further your own.
- When would I need to manipulate someone?

Most times, you may not get what you want in life if you are not ready to take some necessary steps in manipulating other people involved in the process. It is challenging to get what you desire if you are not exactly a careful manipulator. Therefore, you need to learn the necessary steps to use in manipulating people. These steps will surely give you an edge over others because you will know how to appeal to their conscience and mentality without being caught in the act, which may annoy them.

Let us make an analysis of these steps, which involves using body language expressions and spoken words such as:

Manipulative Looks and Stares

Manipulative looks and stares include wearing of stony faces suggesting displeasure and anger over an incident or something else, death stares used for intimidating others, sexy looks and stares intended to seduce and lure a person into sexual intimacy, maintaining eye contact with someone without saying anything, rolling of eyes, and many others.

Shouting Down on Someone or Yelling

Insidious or manipulative persons have a way of using these tactics to cow and frighten their victims. Shouting down on someone or yelling at people is a manipulative tendency aimed at making the other person or persons shut up in fear and condescend to your whims and caprices unconsciously. Mostly, bosses use this manipulative tendency or traits in the offices to suppress anger and maintain control or leadership of the firm. In some cases, the staffs are never comfortable whenever the boss is around; everybody whisks away in fear of the next reprimanding action that may happen.

Manipulations by Avoiding you at All Means

When someone avoids or ignores you, by all means, something is possibly wrong in your relationship with that person. This type of attitude manifests in so many ways such as when someone leaves a meeting when you enter, if a person does not acknowledge your presence in a place but acknowledges others, no response to your e-mails, phone calls, and messages. Moreover, if a person avoids eye contact with you, you should know that something is fishing and beware of interactions with such persons.

Preferential or Silent Treatment

One of the ways to manipulate someone to give what you want is by showing them unusual, preferred, or silent treatment. After giving them this type of attention and care, the chances are that they must succumb to your wishes and desires.

Playing on the Emotions

Master manipulators like to play on your emotions to coerce you to give them what they want from you. They know that if they can make you have a feeling for them, you will surely respond to their requests. Therefore, they look for words and expressions that can captivate your feelings and thoughts to give them a leeway into your heart. These manipulators may use words such as "I love you," or anything that can endear them to you. This attitude is to get what they want from you.

Chapter 8: Victims of Manipulation

Three Ways of Becoming the Victim of a Controlling Manipulator

We have looked at the character of the controlling manipulator, but what of their victims, how do they become ensnared? It might surprise you how much we are all manipulated in our daily lives.

There are situations where any one of us could find ourselves being easily persuaded. Every day we are bombarded with advertisements, all urging us to buy their wares. Extolling the virtues of one product over another. Building a discourse where not buying certain goods is almost seen as unthinkable, out of sync with the zeitgeist.

1. Sales Tactics

This is the obvious example of such a situation. It seems to be the acceptable face of social manipulation. Commercial products always seem to carry some type of manipulative tactic. All in aid of getting the public to buy the goods. The worse of it is that we are aware of the scheming maneuvers, and yet we still fall prey to them.

When marketing is done well, it works. That's why advertising is a multi-million-dollar enterprise. Companies do not have huge advertising budgets for no reason. For example, how often do we succumb to their "Buy One Get One Free" offers or half-price sales? They seem like a real bargain, saving our hard-earned bucks. Often, we are coerced into buying products we might not even need or ever wanted in the first place. The offer tempts us with generous words, such as "Free" or "Reduced." Yet, it is a marketing ploy to manipulate customers to empty out their purses and wallets. It even has its own acronym, known as BOGOF. Customers are seduced by attractive false pretenses. Are the stores or companies really being kind in giving us free products? How can they afford that? The truth of it is that they are not giving anything away for free.

Economist, Alex Tabbarok,* informs us that there are many ways that these offers can seduce us. The cost of a product is seemingly reduced, giving the customer an offer that's too good to refuse. Most likely the price of the product is increased before the offer, so the customer pays more in the first place. Most larger shops buy their goods in bulk. This means that the price they pay for an individual product is far less than the price they charge their customers. That is acceptable because they are a business after all, and must make profits to keep going.

You may also note that the BOGOF temptation is used on a lot of perishable items. If the stores have a surplus and the sell-by date is fast approaching, it makes commercial sense to reduce the price, or use BOGOF. If you are coerced into buying this type of bargain, make sure you can eat it all before it expires. Some have argued that this practice of promotion has led to an increase in food waste. The stores and shops refute this theory completely.

Such commercial practices are seen as choices that adults can assess intelligently. No one is forcing us to participate in the offers. We all have individual agency and should take responsibility for our actions. Yet, somehow, we are blinded to the persuasiveness of such marketing methods.

We live in a consumerist society. The need to own the latest gadget or have the latest model can become crucial to the buyer. Not only for their standing in society but also their sense of self. Advertisers take advantage of our weak areas and offer us unmissable deals at supposedly low rates. If customers cannot afford it, no problem, they will be offered credit for their purchase.

It should come as no surprise that advertising has such a powerful impact on our lives. Linked to the massive increase in consumerism over the last few decades is a similar increase in marketing efforts. In the 1970s, it was believed that the average person viewed around 500 adverts, which has now increased to 5000 ads, in a single day. Whilst that might seem excessive and may not apply to everyone, it does show the pervasive nature of advertising in everyday life. Advertising is proven to work, overtly manipulating the shopper and often tagging into their emotions to coercing them to purchase the product in question. Though it may not work every time and on every person, it is successful often enough to make it a profitable venture.

Of course, no one is physically or mentally abusing customers, or attempting to ruin their lives. It is a business tactic, not a personal ploy. Even though it is done subtly, it can have a powerful effect on the lives and well-being of individuals.

Some people are far more vulnerable to manipulation than others. Some are very impressionable, and sometimes vulnerable too. A classic target for scammers and strong-armed sales personnel are the elderly. They are easy to confuse when a strong character is knocking on their door. This part of the population is perfect for the controlling manipulator. Their weaknesses can be taken advantage of. Such people will not fully comprehend what is being put to them. Even if they do understand, they may fear to say "no." That makes them the perfect target for unscrupulous manipulators.

2. Working Environment

Anyone vulnerable is a potential target of a manipulator. It is not always the obvious people that can get ensnared. Already we have learned that such a character will initially behave with impeccable manners. This false front is performed to impress and gain trust. If you do not know this person already, it may be hard to recognize that you have become their target. That is until it is too late. On a personal front, this type of relationship can occur at work, or even in intimate relationships.

Consider your place of work. Do you have a boss that makes your life a misery by demanding work at higher and quicker levels constantly? Browbeating you to meet impossible targets. Warning you of a reduction in your salary or canceling any bonuses. Could even threaten to sack you. At that point, you become trapped. This person knows we all have responsibilities, such as mortgages or rents, and families to support. We cannot walk away. In such a situation, any of us could become this vulnerable person. This is the victim of a controlling manipulator.

Here are some typical manipulative tactics of this character. See if any sounds familiar in your current work situation. "Careerizma" is a career website that provides useful guidance and resources. In a relevant blog article, they cover this exact topic.

Fake Praise

The boss said they liked your idea and think you're a great person, but then they go with someone else's idea instead. What was the point of the pretense in the first place? Like many manipulators, they like the feeling of control. By leading you astray, it gives them a sense of power over you. This is about building a person's confidence up with false praise and then crushing them. At this point, they may belittle you or devalue your work. Diving in with the kill to make you feel worthless. Now they have you like a puppet under their control.

Stealing the Credit of Your Talents

Using you to write up their own reports, and then taking all the credit for it. This is a classic manipulative strategy. They tell you that you're perfect for the job. Show you how they trust in you as the best person to get the job done. All that encouragement was a complete front for their real plans. Once the job is completed, they claim any praise for themselves. Now you are left on the sideline, feeling well and truly exasperated. Should you question them about it, they'll claim your report was a total mess. It's better now because they spent all morning putting it right.

Embarrassing You

Putting people down, in front of others, makes these characters feel powerful. Say that you put forward an idea, they may laugh and ridicule the very thought of it. After a while, you no longer believe in it yourself. Were you to confront them about their behavior, they' would come back at you with sarcasm, "Hell, man, can't you take a joke?" Cruel jokes and sarcasm all will be done at your expense.

Blame Shifting

Whatever has gone wrong is everyone else's fault, but theirs. Never would they admit up to their own shortcomings and mistakes. Not only that, they'll often deny any negative things they might have done. Should you attempt to explain the wrong they did, they would only claim that your version of events is wrong. Typically, they will say, 'I don't normally behave like that, only when I'm around you." This is what Freud called projection. They are projecting their own misdemeanors onto someone else.

Belittling

Making others feel irrelevant. Such as, if you walk into their office, they don't stop whatever they're doing to greet you. Instead, you get a wave of the hand to come in. They know you are there, but take an age to get to you. It leaves you sitting there feeling insignificant, which is exactly how they want you to feel.

Quite often they will bring irrelevant information into an argument, especially if they are losing. Moving goalposts whilst in a discussion is a classical way to make them look good. These people must have the last word, always.

Unappreciative of anything you do and pushing you to your limits are all signs to watch out for. If you hear these bells, you are working for a manipulative controller.

Working with such people can be a game of survival, and not everyone has the strength of character to win. Some, once they've identified them, will stay clear of such people. Their tactic is to keep them out of their lives by avoiding them. That can be difficult if the person doing the manipulation is your employer or your partner. Others may stand up to them and confront them. This is risky but done in the right way could result in the manipulator moving on to another target. Most of the time we have no choice other than to put up with them. We all have our own strategies on how to deal with people we don't like, but the handling of narcissistic manipulator takes courage.

Working with a controlling figure can make your life unhappy; living with one can make your life hell. Have a look at some of the signs to look out for, to know if you are in such a relationship.

3. Personal Relationships

This is a terrible situation to find you in. Being in a relationship whereby your supposedly loving partner keeps you on a leash. When someone wants to control everything that you do, it can become a dangerous situation to find yourself in. This type of partner might tell you it's for your own good. They are keeping you safe under their protective wing. Yet, being on the other end of such treatment does not feel safe. It is a suffocating experience that comes with other serious problems, such as sexual, physical, and mental abuse.

Chapter 9: Identifying Manipulator Types

Have you ever felt a sudden lack of self-confidence or, worse, this curious and agonizing impression of not knowing how to communicate? Have you ever been deafened by doubt about your skills or qualities? Have you ever been inhabited by that feeling of inferiority that paralyzes you, chills your blood, and prevents you from reacting normally? If you have ever experienced this kind of situation, it is because you have been the victim of type III manipulation and placed in the line of sight of a manipulator.

We remember that the second type of manipulator is a selfish or egocentric person who thinks only of his interests, without worrying about the consequences. But the type III manipulator, which is also called the manipulator, has a very different characteristic intention. His only goal is to destroy. Everything he undertakes is meant to kill you, to ruin what you do, or to destroy an aspect of your personality that does not suit him.

The manipulator is characterized both by his will to harm and by a formidable ability to conceal. This is why many people do not trust him or take him for another.

The manipulator does not display distinctive signs and his perversity does not necessarily read on his face. He is a true chameleon that hides behind deceptive appearances to destroy better. He can take the appearance of a parent who is "overprotective" and who, out of selfishness, prevents his child from becoming independent. The manipulator could be a nice grandmother who, secretly, gives money to her little girl who is in rehab to, supposedly, "help her hold on." It can also be a mistress, a lover, a boss, a neighbor, a teacher, or a long-time friend. In the cozy atmosphere of the offices, it is the collaborator willing to do anything to take your place or that colleague who seeks to devalue you because your expertise is shady.

He intends to destroy. Sometimes it may bring him something, but in this case, it's a secondary benefit because what he's essentially aiming for is the destruction of who you are, what you do, or the other of your behaviors.

Illustration

It is through these situations and testimonies that we will examine the harmful activity of a type III manipulator.

A man wanted his son, Jean, to succeed him by also becoming a doctor at all costs. When Jean announced his desire to leave school to become a musician, his father did everything to break that dream and bring his son back to what he thought was the right path. He tried to persuade his son that he was right in seeking to destroy this vocation. "I did it for your sake, you'll thank me later," he told him then. But what he put his son through was a terrible ordeal that almost drove Jean to suicide, as he felt rejected, devalued, ridiculed, humiliated, and disavowed deep within himself.

A husband insidiously belittles his wife, Christelle, so that she stays at home. He has nothing against her. He simply does not want her to become independent because it's not how things are done in his family and he earns enough to make her happy. As she does not agree, he will do everything to prove (by demeaning and humiliating her) that she is unable to do without him. From his point of view, he thinks he is acting justly and in the interest of his wife. But one can easily imagine that Christelle does not see things in the same way.

A department head, who confronts and belittles a better-performing collaborator than himself, does not necessarily feel particular hatred toward this person. He is simply trying to break the person because he feels they are a danger to him and the only way he can defend his own mediocrity is to belittle them, to diminish them, or to put him in his place so that he does not do not encroach on the department head's work. He destroys what seems to him to be a threat that could prevent him from continuing to dominate the situation. In return, the employee can talk about bullying.

The type III manipulator is a weak man who, when he feels he is in danger, tries to diminish others. He advances masked. Where a normal person tries to surpass himself to become stronger (than whatever threatens him), the manipulator has no other resource than to weaken or treacherously destroy everything that worries him.

He destroys for the sake of destruction. He is mean and does not allow others to exist on their own. He wants to control everything. We cannot impress him. It makes you feel that you are small, weak, and shabby; it turns you into a "mop," it tramples you and makes you incapable of any development.

He destroys you by giving you the impression that it is for your good, but we feel very bad in his presence. We cannot win. We are not recognized for what we would like to be. He does not listen to you, and his criticism is never constructive. When he says something, it's always negative. With him, one feels humiliated, discouraged, and degraded. He is a "mental assassin" and life with him is like slavery.

This test separates the appearance and truth of the situation and highlights the perverse maneuvers that the manipulator uses against us.

Harassment and Concealed Manipulation

Type III manipulation often goes unnoticed by those who experience it. This is called harassment or hidden manipulation. A large number of victims are thus abused and destroyed without their knowledge by the deceit and duplicity of a manipulator. After two pregnancies, Chloe cannot seem to get back to the weight she was as a young girl. She explains her fight against the pounds:

"When I discover a new diet, I hasten to try it. I am sure this time it will be the right one. I do what it takes, and I feel good. I have a clear mind, I am dynamic. Sometimes I even go back to playing sports. I do everything I can without effort and I start losing weight. And then, brutally, without my understanding why, I fall back into the fog. I have no courage, I ruminate on the same black thoughts, I do not do anything, I am exhausted, and I spend my time sleeping. Then, seeing all the tasks accumulating around the apartment, I feel guilty and without realizing it, I start eating again. I call myself names while looking at my belly and my thighs in the mirror of the bathroom. Every day, I decided that, the next day, I will put myself firmly on the diet and that this time I will get there. Today, I am completely desperate because despite all my attempts, every time I get on the scale, I can see that I still gained weight."

While a hidden manipulation is hardly perceptible from the inside, this is not the case when we observe it from the outside. This is what a friend of Chloe tells us about her weight problems:

"I have known Chloe for many years. She was always a little concerned about her weight, but it almost became an obsession from the moment she met Guillaume, her future husband. He is a charming boy, but he attaches great importance to appearances. Since Chloe gained a little weight, having had her children, he frequently comments on it. He always comments nicely, in the tone of the joke, but I think it comes a little too often. I also see that Chloe is touched, even if she pretends to laugh with the others about her 'little bulges' as she says. But I can see that deep down she is hurt when he makes fun of her in public. Moreover, in the days that follow, she regularly buys clothes that are too small, claiming that she is going to lose weight. The other night, I was at home and he did not stop criticizing a common friend who had grown enormously. He told multiple bad jokes about his plumpness and talked about the contempt he had for people who do not know how to control their weight. When Chloe came out of the room with tears in her eyes, he suddenly changed the subject of conversation. Everyone was embarrassed, but he did not seem to notice. The worst part was that he seemed satisfied with what he had just done as if it were a good joke. I thought about Chloe and it was really awful to see how happy he looked."

A manipulator can be extremely pleasant and user-friendly. By appearing charming, playing on someone's guild, or using a respectable or simply authoritarian position, he creates a mirage that deceives his victims and prevents them from seeing that behind his disguise of the moment, hides a purpose that is invariably destructive and harmful. Moreover, it is very difficult to blame him for the behavior because he always has an excuse to justify himself: "I am only following the instructions. I do not have the right to disobey. I only did my duty. I acted believing it was the right thing to do. It was a joke."

To be sure, we can examine (below) the two sets of symptoms that signify the presence of a manipulator. The first contains the essentials of what one feels when one is a direct victim of a manipulator and the second enumerates what one perceives as a mere observer of a hidden manipulation.

Internal Symptoms of Concealed Manipulation

These are the main internal signals that can be seen when one is a victim of type III manipulation. These symptoms are far more indicative of the presence of a manipulator than the analysis of his words or deeds:

- I alternate moments of enthusiasm and discouragement. I often feel a sense of guilt or doubt.
- I find it difficult to defend myself or counterattack. I feel a sudden loss of confidence in myself.
- I sometimes feel that I am "drained" of my energy. I feel physical or mental discomfort in the presence of someone.
- That person belittles me one way or another. It is impossible to impress or affect her.

- There is always a form of ambiguity between what she does and what she says. I am not well in my head or in my body when I am around that person.

If you have at least three symptoms, there is a good chance that you have been the victim of such manipulation. When all five symptoms are reached, manipulation is certain, and you should focus on finding out for sure who the manipulator is and how he proceeds.

Do not hesitate to ask for advice or help!

Generally, someone with an outside perspective can find out much more easily because they will often notice things that one who is a victim and who lives things from within misses.

Final Thoughts on Manipulation

This information gathered by our senses is crucial in the decision-making process of every individual. To gain access to this, one must learn how to read body language cues effectively. Moreover, manipulators take this opportunity to blur the lines by utilizing statements that either limit or expand the choices you see about a particular decision that you have to make.

Other people often pose hurdles to us. They may try to hurt us. They may lie to us, or detect our lies, and try to get us in trouble. They may say no to something that you want or need. But dark psychology allows you to plow through the blockages and hurdles that others create so that you can get anything that you want. You now know how to get your way, no matter what anyone tries to tell you.

Your knowledge of dark psychology is something that most people won't want you to have. You can use this knowledge to become an absolute monster if you so choose. Hopefully, you will use your conscience and avoid employing these methods for evil. Instead, you will use these methods for good. You will become a ninja at getting your way, and you will always have good intentions. You can use these methods to build healthier relationships, bring about organizational change at work, and influence people to do right rather than wrong. You don't have to use them for evil purposes and destroy lives with them. Of course, it is entirely up to you how you use what you have learned.

However, you choose to use this knowledge, you now have a lot of power over others. You can get your way in any situation, with any person. You can influence and change people, molding them into your slaves, metaphorically or literally. You can change your life and pave the way to your own success. How you choose to use this power can affect your karma, so be careful.

From here on out, resolve to treat yourself kindly by associating with kind people, and being decent yourself. Surrounding yourself with positive people who are not high in dark triad traits or cutting off relationships with those who use CEM tactics can be the biggest favor you ever do for.

Using a mix of psychological tells and body language, you will never be at a loss as to what people are thinking. The key part of successful lives is relationships, and now you have the skills to form them. Employ these skills and your friends and work colleagues will notice the change immediately.

Put the techniques that you have learned into practice out in the real world. Find a target that you want to manipulate and try some of your favorite techniques out, whether that means trying to control the narrative, attempting to manage your target's expectations, or making an effort to manipulate your target's beliefs. Do not expect to get everything right the first time and do not be afraid of failure; if something goes wrong, simply learn what you can from the experience and move on to the next target. Learning a new skill is always a process, and that includes learning how to manipulate people in the world around you.

Conclusion

Throughout this book, we have discussed how present manipulation is in all aspects of our lives, including marketing, politics, and our friends and family. We are aware of how politicians and businessmen use these tactics to gain power and authority in our society. We also learned that you can use these tactics to your own advantage. You need to be observant in every social situation to help you become more aware of the manipulative tactics of those around you. Fortunately, after reading this book, you will have the qualifications necessary to identify and read body language and use that information to your advantage.

The main objective of this book is to show you the power you have to become a master of secret manipulative techniques, all you need to do is take control of your own mind. If you are in control of how you think and react, no one will be able to use manipulation against you. You are also more than able to control and persuade those around you by using your mind. Once you have achieved self-realization, you will have achieved the skills necessary to use persuasion to propel you further up the social strata. Remember that you can only have control over others if you have control over yourself.

www.ingramcontent.com/pod-product-compliance
Lightning Source LLC
Chambersburg PA
CBHW062140100526
44589CB00014B/1635